CLOSE——

Your Eyes and Listen

Words Of Inspiration From The Holy Spirit

Jacqueline Stewart

Graphics, Art, and Designs Living Water Books

A MOTHER'S LOVE

Chauncey, in my heart, you will always be that little boy who so quickly became a strong, loving, and kind young man. I was honored to be your mother. You brought so much joy and happiness to my life. I am forever grateful for the time God allowed us to share and the memories we created. The words you spoke to me, "Mom just Smile" will forever burn bright in my heart.

Your Wings were ready; however, My Heart was not I love you more than words could ever say, and I miss you even more. You will never be forgotten! Missing you, along with the peace and calm you brought in my life. Your loving spirit will always be with us, reminding us to enjoy life with each other and find joy in the small moments. Loving you always. Mom, Donyada, and Marquis.

*I am a seed
preparing to grow
into divine fruit.*

JACQUELINE STEWART

This devotional belongs to

_____

James 1:22

"Don't just hear God's Word but obey it."

When I close my eyes and listen,
Lord...... I see and hear you!

When the natural eyes are closed to
this world, then the spiritual eyes
are open to Heaven!

CONTENTS _____
Daily Devotional of Friendship

CONTENTS _____
Daily Devotional of Friendship

CONTENTS _____

Daily Devotional of Friendship

Emergency Numbers

Choose from the option below, any number is available for you to close your eyes and listen.

Face with Sorrow.. John 14

When Man fails you .... Psalm 27

When you feel like a failure ....Psalm 51

When you are worried .... Matthew 6:19-34

Feeling scared or in danger .... Psalm 91

If God seems far away .... Hebrews 13:9

Needing to increase in faith .... Hebrews 11

Feeling lonely or fearful .... Hebrew 13:5

Needing Peace and Rest .... Matthew 11:25-30

Needing Courage .... Joshua 1

Deciding on a divine opportunity .... Isaiah 55

Needing a financial blessing .... Psalm 37

Discouraged about work .... Psalm 126

Need a Friend .... John 15:15

*I am the sound
surrounding you.
You must listen with your
eyes and see with your
ears!*

DayOne

Dear Beloved,

I need you to hear my voice, obey, and understand that my love has been with you in all your ways. All I want is your true worship. Please allow me to pour my love into you so that you may be able to pour it into others.

Many hearts have waxed cold and no longer see me as the promise. Don't be a part of that number. Turn from the wickedness that interferes. My word is your guide to live more abundantly. I am love and I love you! Trust my ways and follow me.

Close your eyes and Listen

Jesus told his disciples, "The Holy Spirit, whom the Father will send in my name, He will teach you all things and bring to your remembrance all that I have said to you" (John 14:26, ESV).

Today the Holy Spirit said:

_____

_____

_____

_____

_____

_____

_____

_____

_____

Application:

_____

_____

_____

_____

Water your mind with positive thoughts and
watch beautiful flowers of greatness grow.

Your days will be long lived and your best days are on the way.

JACQUELINE STEWART

DayTwo

Dear Beloved,

I am here for you even when you don't think that I am. I heard your prayers asking for forgiveness, and I have cleansed you from all your sins. All that seek to hurt you have no power because I am your fortress. Remember that you are a new creature in Christ. Your heart is pure and clean before me.

I will always lead and guide you by my spirit. Beloved, remember the tree is never moved, no matter what is going on.

Close your eyes and Listen

Jesus told his disciples, "The Holy Spirit, whom the Father will send in my name, He will teach you all things and bring to your remembrance all that I have said to you" (John 14:26, ESV).

Today the Holy Spirit said:

_____

_____

_____

_____

_____

_____

_____

_____

_____

_____

Application:

_____

_____

_____

_____

Water your mind with positive thoughts and
watch beautiful flowers of greatness grow

I came into this world with a purpose I will fulfill.

JACQUELINE STEWART

DayThree

Dear Beloved,

Sometimes there are no words just tears in your prayer time. I feel you and I am the pillow for your tears. I know your every thought just quiet your soul and listen.

I want you to use the measure of faith I have given to you. Get to know me as I know you and your faith will carry you. I know you are afraid but I am with you. Can you imagine walking in my shadow, as i step... you step? You have taken a major step of faith by coming to me, now let me walk you through it. I am here for you!

21

Close your eyes and Listen

Jesus told his disciples, "The Holy Spirit, whom the Father will send in my name, He will teach you all things and bring to your remembrance all that I have said to you" (John 14:26, ESV).

Today the Holy Spirit said:

_____

_____

_____

_____

_____

_____

_____

_____

_____

Application:

_____

_____

_____

_____

*Water your mind with positive thoughts
and watch beautiful flowers of greatness grow*

*Water your mind with positive thoughts
and watch beautiful flowers of greatness grow*

Water your mind with positive thoughts
and watch beautiful flowers of greatness grow

*Trust my lead
and rest in peace.*

JACQUELINE STEWART

Day Four

Dear Beloved,

When you close your eyes? Do you feel me in your heart? Do you feel the cool breeze as my shadow passes over you? Do you feel my touch as you worship me? I am clinging to you! My presence is in your home, and in your heart. I call upon you and walk with you into a luscious land of love.

You are my beloved, and my will for you is perfect. Please know that you mean everything to me.

Close your eyes and Listen

Jesus told his disciples, "The Holy Spirit, whom the Father will send in my name, He will teach you all things and bring to your remembrance all that I have said to you" (John 14:26, ESV).

Today the Holy Spirit said:

_____

_____

_____

_____

_____

_____

_____

_____

_____

_____

Application:

_____

_____

_____

_____

Water your mind with positive thoughts
and watch beautiful flowers of greatness grow

Water your mind with positive thoughts
and watch beautiful flowers of greatness grow

Water your mind with positive thoughts
and watch beautiful flowers of greatness grow

The father is with you wherever you go and he watches over you!

JACQUELINE STEWART

Day Five

Dear Beloved,

I will heal you and this land once you turn your heart back to me. I am a jealous God, and I will have no one before me.

I want you to know that you are important to me, and my love for you will never cease. My arms are open for you; now run to me. No matter how hard or bad the pain is, just know I have carried all your pain. I am your God.

Close your eyes and Listen

Jesus told his disciples, "The Holy Spirit, whom the Father will send in my name, He will teach you all things and bring to your remembrance all that I have said to you" (John 14:26, ESV).

Today the Holy Spirit said:

_____

_____

_____

_____

_____

_____

_____

_____

_____

Application:

_____

_____

_____

_____

Water your mind with positive thoughts
and watch beautiful flowers of greatness grow

Water your mind with positive thoughts
and watch beautiful flowers of greatness grow

*Water your mind with positive thoughts
and watch beautiful flowers of greatness grow*

You will find love
When you find
God and truly give
Him your heart.

JACQUELINE STEWART

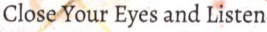

Day Six

Dear Beloved,

I am so attentive to your heart and the way you speak out of it. No one else knows you as I do. My love for you is unconditional. I need you to worship and praise me in this moment as you let me lead you into the land of abundance! Allow me to help you become who I have destined you to be!

My promise is sure, and I will not lead you astray. I will give you rest, peace, and a covering. I want you to seek me with your whole heart and hide in me.

Close your eyes and Listen

Jesus told his disciples, "The Holy Spirit, whom the Father will send in my name, He will teach you all things and bring to your remembrance all that I have said to you" (John 14:26, ESV).

Today the Holy Spirit said:

_____

_____

_____

_____

_____

_____

_____

_____

_____

_____

Application:

_____

_____

_____

_____

*Water your mind with positive thoughts
and watch beautiful flowers of greatness grow*

*You are the light
that brightens
every life around you!*

JACQUELINE STEWART

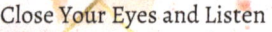

Day Seven

Dear Beloved,

I have sent the rain to renew and refresh your mind so that you may be able to hear me and only me. I am here to take care of you. Just put it in the atmosphere now, and I will draw near to you!

I am your healer, supplier, lawyer, lender, and provider. I am your everything for any season. Please cast all of your cares on me because love is waiting to lavish joy on you in the place of your pain.

Close your eyes and Listen

Jesus told his disciples, "The Holy Spirit, whom the Father will send in my name, He will teach you all things and bring to your remembrance all that I have said to you" (John 14:26, ESV).

Today the Holy Spirit said:

_____

_____

_____

_____

_____

_____

_____

_____

Application:

_____

_____

_____

_____

Water your mind with positive thoughts
and watch beautiful flowers of greatness grow

Water your mind with positive thoughts
and watch beautiful flowers of greatness grow

*Water your mind with positive thoughts
and watch beautiful flowers of greatness grow*

You are already victorious! Keep the faith and trust God.

JACQUELINE STEWART

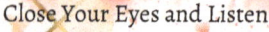

Day Eight

Dear Beloved,

I am here, destiny is here for you! I have allowed you to go through all that you have gone through to see you emerge as the one I have pre-destined from the beginning.

I took no delight in seeing you cry but welcomed the newness of life each moment brought forth. You will reach your destiny, and I will clear your mind of anything that doesn't line up with me. Don't forget that today is a day designed for you!

Close your eyes and Listen

Jesus told his disciples, "The Holy Spirit, whom the Father will send in my name, He will teach you all things and bring to your remembrance all that I have said to you" (John 14:26, ESV).

Today the Holy Spirit said:

_____

_____

_____

_____

_____

_____

_____

_____

_____

_____

Application:

_____

_____

_____

_____

*Water your mind with positive thoughts
and watch beautiful flowers of greatness grow*

Water your mind with positive thoughts
and watch beautiful flowers of greatness grow

Water your mind with positive thoughts
and watch beautiful flowers of greatness grow

*I came into this world
with a purpose.*

JACQUELINE STEWART

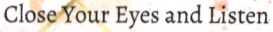

Day Nine

Dear Beloved,

I am honored to be your first love and your priority. I am so pleased with your worship and the way your heart yields to mine! Ask, and you shall receive, beloved! If you seek me with your whole heart, you shall find me, and along with me, you'll find the desires of your heart.

Don't try to rush the way my WORD develops within you. Just rest in the promises and become one with them. It is my desire for you to grow!

Close your eyes and Listen

Jesus told his disciples, "The Holy Spirit, whom the Father will send in my name, He will teach you all things and bring to your remembrance all that I have said to you" (John 14:26, ESV).

Today the Holy Spirit said:

_____

_____

_____

_____

_____

_____

_____

_____

_____

Application:

_____

_____

_____

_____

*Water your mind with positive thoughts
and watch beautiful flowers of greatness grow*

*Water your mind with positive thoughts
and watch beautiful flowers of greatness grow*

Water your mind with positive thoughts
and watch beautiful flowers of greatness grow

*I am believing
in God for everything.*

JACQUELINE STEWART

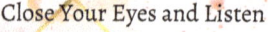

Day Ten

Dear Beloved,

Let my will be done in your life, whatever you do or become a part of, matters to me. Let your light so shine that I may speak the truth through you and shine in the lives of others. I want others to see your good works and glorify me!

Will you be in close partnership with me? Speak to me within your heart and say. Lord, your Kingdom come, your will be done, on earth as it is in Heaven. I will show up for you and override your situation!

61

Close your eyes and Listen

Jesus told his disciples, "The Holy Spirit, whom the Father will send in my name, He will teach you all things and bring to your remembrance all that I have said to you" (John 14:26, ESV).

Today the Holy Spirit said:

_____

_____

_____

_____

_____

_____

_____

_____

_____

_____

Application:

_____

_____

_____

_____

*Water your mind with positive thoughts and watch
beautiful flowers of greatness grow*

Water your mind with positive thoughts and watch
beautiful flowers of greatness grow

My faith keeps me
focused on God.

JACQUELINE STEWART

Day Eleven

Dear Beloved,

I am here for you even when you don't think that I am. I heard your prayers, and I have cleansed you from all your sins. You are a new creature in Christ. Your heart is clean, and you're now ready to step out on faith.

Don't turn to the east, west, north, or south. Turn to me, look within, and live. I am within you. I will lead and guide you by my spirit. Beloved, remember the tree is not moved, no matter what is going on.

Close your eyes and Listen

Jesus told his disciples, "The Holy Spirit, whom the Father will send in my name, He will teach you all things and bring to your remembrance all that I have said to you" (John 14:26, ESV).

Today the Holy Spirit said:

_____

_____

_____

_____

_____

_____

_____

_____

Application:

_____

_____

_____

_____

*Water your mind with positive thoughts and
watch beautiful flowers of greatness grow*

Water your mind with positive thoughts and watch beautiful flowers of greatness grow

Water your mind with positive thoughts and watch beautiful flowers of greatness grow

*God's love reminds
me that I am
whole and Complete*

JACQUELINE STEWART

Day Twelve

Dear Beloved,

I will strengthen you through every issue that you have to face, and I will restore all that has been taken away from you. I will give you beauty for ashes, and I will make your crooked roads straight.

It brings me joy to turn your sadness into joy. I will give you the wisdom to run the race before you. I know you think you're at the end of your trail but your journey has just begun.

Close your eyes and Listen

Jesus told his disciples, "The Holy Spirit, whom the Father will send in my name, He will teach you all things and bring to your remembrance all that I have said to you" (John 14:26, ESV).

Today the Holy Spirit said:

_____

_____

_____

_____

_____

_____

_____

_____

Application:

_____

_____

_____

_____

Water your mind with positive thoughts and watch
beautiful flowers of greatness grow

Water your mind with positive thoughts and watch
beautiful flowers of greatness grow

*I am the salt
of the earth and I season
the lives of many.*

JACQUELINE STEWART

Day Thirteen

Dear Beloved,

You've seen my mighty works, and this is only the beginning. Just as my mighty hand worked through Moses to accomplish the purpose, so then shall my hand be upon you.

My purpose was not only to rescue the Hebrews but also to teach them about my character.

Close your eyes and Listen

Jesus told his disciples, "The Holy Spirit, whom the Father will send in my name, He will teach you all things and bring to your remembrance all that I have said to you" (John 14:26, ESV).

Today the Holy Spirit said:

_____

_____

_____

_____

_____

_____

_____

_____

Application:

_____

_____

_____

_____

Water your mind with positive thoughts
and watch beautiful flowers of greatness grow

Water your mind with positive thoughts and watch
beautiful flowers of greatness grow

*Water your mind with positive thoughts and watch
beautiful flowers of greatness grow*

*Jesus loves me
and chose me for
greater.*

JACQUELINE STEWART

Day Fourteen

Dear Beloved,

Fret not, for I have you. I needed to know if you truly trusted me for your needs to be met, so I allowed you to go through some things. I am building character within you. You are a leader chosen by me, but before you were a leader, you were always my child.

I want you to remember that no weapon formed against you shall prosper. Look for my signs and wonders all around you. My favor is upon you; just stand still and watch me work on your behalf. You shall never be broke another day in your life, just don't forget to bless me first. All your needs will be met just as I did before.

Close your eyes and Listen

Jesus told his disciples, "The Holy Spirit, whom the Father will send in my name, He will teach you all things and bring to your remembrance all that I have said to you" (John 14:26, ESV).

Today the Holy Spirit said:

_____

_____

_____

_____

_____

_____

_____

_____

Application:

_____

_____

_____

_____

Water your mind with positive thoughts and watch beautiful flowers of greatness grow

*Water your mind with positive thoughts and watch
beautiful flowers of greatness grow*

He gave me peace
and I will not let
anyone take it from me

JACQUELINE STEWART

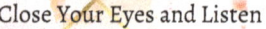

Day Fifteen

Dear Beloved

Iron sharpens iron, and a sweet friendship refreshes the soul. I am your friend, and friends can be the greatest source of love, healing, joy, peace, and encouragement. Be mindful of the kind of people who enter your life! I don't send everyone into your life, but I do allow it and want you to trust me to show you the truth about who you see.

Always seek me with your whole heart. Always listen to my voice and discern when someone else is talking!. I will help you because I am your friend, and those I send will have my spirit!

91

Close your eyes and Listen

Jesus told his disciples, "The Holy Spirit, whom the Father will send in my name, He will teach you all things and bring to your remembrance all that I have said to you" (John 14:26, ESV).

Today the Holy Spirit said:

_____

_____

_____

_____

_____

_____

_____

_____

_____

Application:

_____

_____

_____

_____

Water your mind with positive thoughts and watch
beautiful flowers of greatness grow

Water your mind with positive thoughts and watch
beautiful flowers of greatness grow

Water your mind with positive thoughts and watch beautiful flowers of greatness grow

He lives in me!

JACQUELINE STEWART

Day Sixteen

Dear Beloved.

Close your eyes and listen! Now walk. Don't think, just walk according to the precepts and plans. I will use you to speak to those who are silent because they feel that no one will listen, and they have been overlooked.

I have never looked over you or each of them. I admit sometimes I am silent, but it's not because I am ignoring you. It is because I need you to rest in the last instruction I gave for your life! Don't be so quick to move from one place to the other!

Close your eyes and Listen

Jesus told his disciples, "The Holy Spirit, whom the Father will send in my name, He will teach you all things and bring to your remembrance all that I have said to you" (John 14:26, ESV).

Today the Holy Spirit said:

_____

_____

_____

_____

_____

_____

_____

_____

Application:

_____

_____

_____

_____

Water your mind with positive thoughts and watch
beautiful flowers of greatness grow

Water your mind with positive thoughts and watch
beautiful flowers of greatness grow

*Water your mind with positive thoughts and watch
beautiful flowers of greatness grow*

The battle is not mine, it is the Lord's battle. He has given me angels to protect me. I have angels on my side.

JACQUELINE STEWART

Day Seventeen

Dear Beloved,

I have knitted you together in the womb and brought you this far in your life. From birth to now, where you are, I have already been every step of the way!

One of the most amazing things to focus on is that you have a promise in your heart that I will never leave you nor forsake you! You are chosen by God for such a time as this. Do not underestimate his power over you and how he can turn any situation around for you!

Close your eyes and Listen

Jesus told his disciples, "The Holy Spirit, whom the Father will send in my name, He will teach you all things and bring to your remembrance all that I have said to you" (John 14:26, ESV).

Today the Holy Spirit said:

_____

_____

_____

_____

_____

_____

_____

_____

_____

_____

Application:

_____

_____

_____

_____

Water your mind with positive thoughts and watch
beautiful flowers of greatness grow

Water your mind with positive thoughts and watch beautiful flowers of greatness grow

*Water your mind with positive thoughts and watch
beautiful flowers of greatness grow*

Lord, I need you!

JACQUELINE STEWART

Day Eighteen

Dear Beloved

Close your eyes and listen to the sound of faith erupting from within you! I want you to imagine an earthquake and how even the ground shakes at the movement of the tornado.... the same for your faith in me! I am the sound surrounding you, and you must listen with your eyes and see with your ears!

Know me just as you know the habits of your day! Know me and hear me! Hear my voice, understand, and obey! I have blessings in store for you!

Close your eyes and Listen

Jesus told his disciples, "The Holy Spirit, whom the Father will send in my name, He will teach you all things and bring to your remembrance all that I have said to you" (John 14:26, ESV).

Today the Holy Spirit said:

_____

_____

_____

_____

_____

_____

_____

_____

_____

_____

Application:

_____

_____

_____

_____

Water your mind with positive thoughts and watch
beautiful flowers of greatness grow

Water your mind with positive thoughts and watch beautiful flowers of greatness grow

I trust God with me and I respond to Him in reverence.

JACQUELINE STEWART

Day Nineteen

Dear Beloved,

I have allowed you to rest in this season and it is now time for you to move forward in the things you are passionate about. I will walk you through it all just stay true to yourself at all times and lean not to your own understanding. Keep your eyes open to seek me and your ears open to hear my voice.

The WORD I give to you and leave with you will continue to watch over all that pertains to you. Speak the WORD over yourself, for in doing so you are covering yourself with truth! Truth always prevails despite what others think!

115

Close your eyes and Listen

Jesus told his disciples, "The Holy Spirit, whom the Father will send in my name, He will teach you all things and bring to your remembrance all that I have said to you" (John 14:26, ESV).

Today the Holy Spirit said:

_____

_____

_____

_____

_____

_____

_____

_____

_____

_____

Application:

_____

_____

_____

_____

*Water your mind with positive thoughts and watch
beautiful flowers of greatness grow*

Water your mind with positive thoughts and watch
beautiful flowers of greatness grow

Water your mind with positive thoughts and watch
beautiful flowers of greatness grow

*Ask and it shall
be given unto you.
Trust my will for your life!*

JACQUELINE STEWART

Day Twenty

Dear Beloved,

I will touch the heart of man, and you will see the changes right before your eyes. Fret not because all things are working for your good.

You have given so much, and it is now time for you to receive, watch the tide change on your behalf. I command the wind to blow a fresh start for you in your life just take me at my word. It is your time, my beloved!!!

Close your eyes and Listen

Jesus told his disciples, "The Holy Spirit, whom the Father will send in my name, He will teach you all things and bring to your remembrance all that I have said to you" (John 14:26, ESV).

Today the Holy Spirit said:

_____

_____

_____

_____

_____

_____

_____

_____

_____

_____

Application:

_____

_____

_____

_____

Water your mind with positive thoughts and watch
beautiful flowers of greatness grow

*Water your mind with positive thoughts and watch
beautiful flowers of greatness grow*

Day Twenty One

Dear Beloved,

Close your eyes and listen! Listen to the way I beckon for you! It's time to dream dreams that you cannot achieve on your own! Dreams that only I can awaken, stir, and produce! Dream dreams where you see the heavenly response to an earthly situation!

Dream again! Dream again! Dream again!

Close your eyes and Listen

Jesus told his disciples, "The Holy Spirit, whom the Father will send in my name, He will teach you all things and bring to your remembrance all that I have said to you" (John 14:26, ESV).

Today the Holy Spirit said:

_____

_____

_____

_____

_____

_____

_____

_____

_____

Application:

_____

_____

_____

_____

Water your mind with positive thoughts and watch
beautiful flowers of greatness grow

Water your mind with positive thoughts and watch beautiful flowers of greatness grow

QUOTES ——
And Notes

*I want you to learn
the importance of hearing
from Holy Spirit!*

Write down all that you hear from God.

Close your eyes and Listen

Jesus told his disciples, "The Holy Spirit, whom the Father will send in my name, He will teach you all things and bring to your remembrance all that I have said to you" (John 14:26, ESV).

Today the Holy Spirit said:

_____

_____

_____

_____

_____

_____

_____

_____

_____

Application:

_____

_____

_____

_____

*Seek me first
and I will change
things.*

JACQUELINE STEWART

Close your eyes and Listen

Jesus told his disciples, "The Holy Spirit, whom the Father will send in my name, He will teach you all things and bring to your remembrance all that I have said to you" (John 14:26, ESV).

Today the Holy Spirit said:

_____

_____

_____

_____

_____

_____

_____

_____

_____

Application:

_____

_____

_____

_____

I came into this world with a purpose, and I will fulfill it.

JACQUELINE STEWART

Close your eyes and Listen

Jesus told his disciples, "The Holy Spirit, whom the Father will send in my name, He will teach you all things and bring to your remembrance all that I have said to you" (John 14:26, ESV).

Today the Holy Spirit said:

_____

_____

_____

_____

_____

_____

_____

_____

_____

Application:

_____

_____

_____

_____

I will fight battles that were sent to destroy you. You shall reign!

JACQUELINE STEWART

Close your eyes and Listen

Jesus told his disciples, "The Holy Spirit, whom the Father will send in my name, He will teach you all things and bring to your remembrance all that I have said to you" (John 14:26, ESV).

Today the Holy Spirit said:

_____

_____

_____

_____

_____

_____

_____

_____

_____

Application:

_____

_____

_____

_____

*Let no one take your
God-given joy from you!*

JACQUELINE STEWART

Close your eyes and Listen

Jesus told his disciples, "The Holy Spirit, whom the Father will send in my name, He will teach you all things and bring to your remembrance all that I have said to you" (John 14:26, ESV).

Today the Holy Spirit said:

_____

_____

_____

_____

_____

_____

_____

_____

_____

Application:

_____

_____

_____

I can do all things for you if you allow me to be your source!

JACQUELINE STEWART

Close your eyes and Listen

Jesus told his disciples, "The Holy Spirit, whom the Father will send in my name, He will teach you all things and bring to your remembrance all that I have said to you" (John 14:26, ESV).

Today the Holy Spirit said:

_____

_____

_____

_____

_____

_____

_____

_____

_____

Application:

_____

_____

_____

_____

When you know your value you don't have to beg people to like you!

JACQUELINE STEWART

Close your eyes and Listen

Jesus told his disciples, "The Holy Spirit, whom the Father will send in my name, He will teach you all things and bring to your remembrance all that I have said to you" (John 14:26, ESV).

Today the Holy Spirit said:

_____

_____

_____

_____

_____

_____

_____

_____

_____

Application:

_____

_____

_____

_____

I chose you and choosing you has been my greatest gift to myself!

JACQUELINE STEWART

Close your eyes and Listen

Jesus told his disciples, "The Holy Spirit, whom the Father will send in my name, He will teach you all things and bring to your remembrance all that I have said to you" (John 14:26, ESV).

Today the Holy Spirit said:

_____

_____

_____

_____

_____

_____

_____

_____

_____

Application:

_____

_____

_____

_____

You have been silent long enough ask me for my wisdom so that I can help you fulfill your purpose!

JACQUELINE STEWART

Close your eyes and Listen

Jesus told his disciples, "The Holy Spirit, whom the Father will send in my name, He will teach you all things and bring to your remembrance all that I have said to you" (John 14:26, ESV).

Today the Holy Spirit said:

_____

_____

_____

_____

_____

_____

_____

_____

_____

Application:

_____

_____

_____

_____

A man gives you a job that he can take away, but God gives you work that you've been assigned to complete before the foundations of the earth!

JACQUELINE STEWART

Close your eyes and Listen

Jesus told his disciples, "The Holy Spirit, whom the Father will send in my name, He will teach you all things and bring to your remembrance all that I have said to you" (John 14:26, ESV).

Today the Holy Spirit said:

_____

_____

_____

_____

_____

_____

_____

_____

_____

Application:

_____

_____

_____

_____

He loves you unconditionally and you have special strength available to you through the power of Christ.

JACQUELINE STEWART

Close your eyes and Listen

Jesus told his disciples, "The Holy Spirit, whom the Father will send in my name, He will teach you all things and bring to your remembrance all that I have said to you" (John 14:26, ESV).

Today the Holy Spirit said:

_____

_____

_____

_____

_____

_____

_____

_____

_____

_____

Application:

_____

_____

_____

_____

Close your eyes and Listen

Jesus told his disciples, "The Holy Spirit, whom the Father will send in my name, He will teach you all things and bring to your remembrance all that I have said to you" ([John 14:26](), ESV).

Today the Holy Spirit said:

_____

_____

_____

_____

_____

_____

_____

_____

_____

Application:

_____

_____

_____

_____

A DAUGHTER'S LOVE

To my dad, Louis Howard, I remember as a little girl running down the railroad tracks to meet you. I couldn't tell the time, but I knew what time to run down to that track. When I saw your shadow, I knew what was next. You would always pick me up, twirl me around, and hold me close. You would carry me home, and as I grew into an adult, our thing became punching each other on the arm. You would grab me and say That's enough because it seemed like I could hit harder. You'd tell me you love me.

I hold those words in my heart, waiting for the day when we will hold each other again. My heart was torn when you transitioned, and I struggled with the heartache that came when I knew I would not hear your voice, see your face or punch you again. Close your eyes and listen was inspired by you, my dad because you would always say Close your eyes, you can hear better.

Even now I close my eyes and remember my dad as he twirled me around and carried me safely home. Now he's safely home.

I will always love you Dad.

Thank-you!

To Lisa Bryant
A co-worker who spoke into my life 20-some-odd years ago.... she said that I would write a book!

Lisa, you saw something in me that I didn't see in myself, and to God be the glory. Close your eyes and listen was born. Thank you from the bottom of my heart. and much love to you!

Jacqueline Stewart
thefognonly@gmail.com

Contact

I would like to thank you for ordering my book and supporting the vision God gave to me. It truly has been a journey, but it's well worth it. Sometimes we don't know the gifts we have lying dormant within us until we step out on faith to see what God has created us for. This book is just the beginning of many more gifts streaming from within me. Please let my faith journey encourage you to step out as well!!

Contact

Jacqueline Stewart
thefognonly@gmail.com

"YOU HAVE SUCH A POWERFUL BOOK INSIDE OF YOU"

LIVING WATER BOOKS

Livingwaterbooks.org

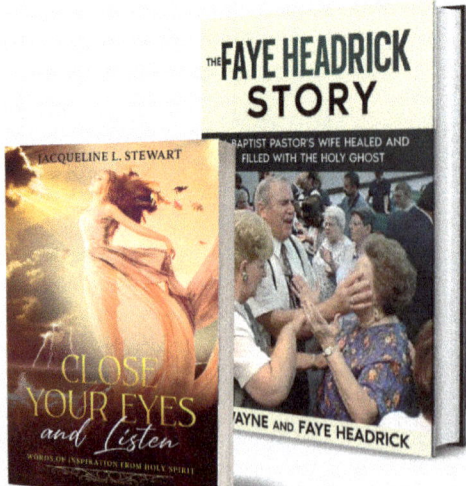

PUBLISHING CO

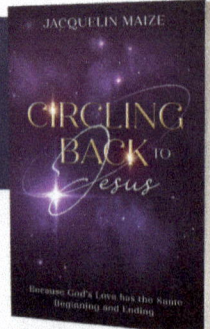

www.ingramcontent.com/pod-product-compliance
Lightning Source LLC
Chambersburg PA
CBHW051526120626
46551CB00012B/1103